A FAMILY PORTRAIT
Memories I Will Never Forget

A Family Portrait

Memories I Will Never Forget

NAIRA BABAYAN
as told to Susan E. Silver

LUMINARE PRESS
WWW.LUMINAREPRESS.COM

A Family Portrait: Memories I Will Never Forget
Copyright © 2020 by Naira Babayan

All rights reserved. This book or any portion thereof may not be reproduced or used in any manner whatsoever without the express written permission of the publisher, except for the use of brief quotations in a book review.

Printed in the United States of America

Cover Design by Claire Flint Last

Luminare Press
442 Charnelton St.
Eugene, OR 97401
www.luminarepress.com

LCCN: 2020904649
ISBN: 978-1-64388-336-6

For my family.

Especially for my parents.
For my father Alfred, whom I lost tragically
at the age of four, but who has always been
in my heart and is protecting me from above.
For my loving mom Ela, who supported me
in the decisions I have made in my life.
And for my lovely daughters Mariam and Joann,
whom I adore and am very proud of.

How I love you all.

Table of Contents

Author's Note ix
Prologue 1
   1. My Dad's Passing 3
   2. Telemak 6
   3. Mother 12
   4. Education 16
   5. Music Conservatory 22
   6. Earthquake 25
   7. Graduation 29
   8. Moscow 31
   9. Albert 35
  10. Dubai 40
  11. Apartment 43
  12. Learning Dubai 45
  13. Living in Dubai 64
  14. Performance 68
  15. Money Matters 71
  16. Back in Armenia 77
  17. Going to the United States 82
  18. Teaching 88
  19. Unknown Pieces by Sergei Rachmaninoff 91
  20. Friends I Have Met 94
  21. Performance at Steinway Piano Gallery 98
Acknowledgments 103

Author's Note

During recent trips to Armenia, I began to look through family albums to remind myself of my life there. Doing so also reminded me of experiences I'd had with various members of my family, and the thought occurred to me to tell my life story and the moments that had a major impact on me.

In this book, I want to share my memories of these experiences and the feelings connected to the loved ones in my life. My aim is to inform the reader of the times and spaces in which these memories originated.

I think the reader will be interested to learn about three generations of an Armenian family, our traditions, and our lifestyles during a particular period of Armenian history.

Prologue

Naira Babayan was born into a prominent Armenian family but lost her father in a tragic accident at an early age. She was very close to her grandparents, especially her grandfather Telemak. Her mother was also a great influence in her life. Recognizing Naira's musical gifts early on, her mother enrolled her in the Tchaikovsky School of Music in Yerevan, Armenia, where Naira excelled as a young pianist. From there, Naira went on to study at the Komitas State Conservatory in Yerevan, then at the Gnessin Academy of Music in Moscow, Russia.

When Armenia became independent from the Soviet Union in 1991, everything changed in Armenia, Naira's life included. With all the new challenges that she faced, Naira realized that her future as a musician could not be fulfilled in Armenia, and she decided to take advantage of opportunities to work and live in the United States. But she never forgot where she came from, and always treasured the memories of her family in Armenia.

This is the story of Naira's triumph over many obstacles and her determination to survive, flourish, and provide a great future for her daughters.

—*Susan E. Silver*

CHAPTER ONE

My Dad's Passing

When my father died on January 24, 1971, I was only four years old, so I was taken away from the house. But my brother remembers those last days at our home, when many important people in the government came to our house. It was wintertime and the days were cold and snowy.

In Armenia, when a person passes away, the family brings the body back to the house. All mirrors and furniture are covered in white linen, and all decorations are covered. The body is placed in the middle of the room on a table, and the relatives surround the casket. At my father's viewing and funeral, Armenian music was playing, and because he was a famous, important government figure, security stood guard next to his coffin. Djivan Gasparyan played his magical duduk (an Armenian national folk instrument) at the viewing and funeral. It was a very moving dedication to his friend Alfred, who met an untimely death.

The week before my father died, my mom and dad attended a wedding in Tbilisi. They had a beautiful time at the wedding, but on the way home, my mom caught a cold and was not feeling well. The next Saturday, my father decided to go to the countryside to celebrate the birthday of one of his friends. As my mother was still not feeling well enough to travel, my father planned to go with a friend. My mother begged him not to go, but my father had promised his friend that he would. He was supposed to return that evening, and my parents were planning to go to the movies after the party.

My mother waited up for him, and it was getting late. There were, of course, no mobile phones at that time. My mom decided to go to bed. She turned the light on to read but soon fell asleep. My grandparents also fell asleep.

It was late and getting dark when my dad left Abovyan City in the Kotayk province, northeast of Yerevan, to return home. On the way back, he stopped at a restaurant for dinner. There, my dad ran into our neighbor, who was with his girlfriend. The neighbor asked my dad to drop him at his (the neighbor's) house.

On the way home from the restaurant, my dad sat in the front seat with his driver. There were three in the back seat: my dad's friend who accompanied him on the trip, the neighbor, and the neighbor's girlfriend. They were driving down a mountain road. A big truck was broken down with its lights off. The driver of my dad's car was tired and fell asleep, and the car slammed into the truck. There were no airbags or seat belts. Four people were killed, including my dad. The girlfriend survived, but her skull came off on impact.

An ambulance arrived. One of the nurses in the ambulance was the sister of my dad's closest friend. It was early morning, around six o'clock, when the doorbell rang. My mom woke up and panicked—my dad was not there beside her. The light was still on. My grandparents woke up and opened the door. My grandmother's brother-in-law and two friends of my dad were standing at the door to deliver the horrible news.

All of Armenia mourned my father's death. All the streets were blocked and everybody cried out loud, even the men.

My father was a unique person. He had adored his parents. At the funeral, my grandmother cried out loud, "How did you do this to us? You promised you would bury us in a gold coffin, and now we are burying you, our only child?!"

A few days before the crash, I had run to my dad, who enveloped me in his arms and said to my mother, "Please take care of my daughter."

My mother replied, "Why do you say that? We both will take care of her."

And my father said, "I know that, but take good care of her."

My mom kept her promise to my dad. A widow at thirty-two, she never remarried, and she stayed in the same house with her in-laws. She sacrificed her life to give us a better life. Education was her first priority for us, to make us good citizens, respect others, and appreciate life.

CHAPTER TWO

Telemak

When I look back, I cherish the days I spent with my grandfather Telemak, my father's father. He was the most loving, caring, devoted person in my life, and I will carry those thoughts with me through the rest of my life.

All the family had lived in Telemak's house before my father died. After my dad's accident, we continued to live together in my grandparents' house. Out of deep love and respect for my father's memory, my mother decided not to change anything in our lives. My best memories are from that time of my life.

Telemak was very parental toward my brother and me. Arthur was eleven years old, seven years older than me, and he especially felt the tragedy of losing his father. And of course, my grandfather had lost his only son.

My grandfather loved to take me to school. He was the first person to wake up in the mornings, around 5:30 or 6:00 a.m. He would walk to the bakery and buy a fresh, warm loaf of matnakash, a typical round Armenian bread, while my grandmother prepared coffee and delicious sweet tea for us on her gas stove. When I woke up around 8:00

a.m.—classes began at 8:30—my grandmother would prepare a hot breakfast for us.

At the table, we would break the matnakash into small pieces and eat it with salty goat cheese. Sometimes we also had oatmeal or eggs. My mother was always concerned that I would gain weight from this rich breakfast.

As executive director of finances for the Parliament of the Republic of Armenia, my grandfather had his own driver. But as a humble man, he would say, "I don't need a driver—I enjoy traveling with my colleagues. I'll take a bus along with the rest of the people."

The bus that carried all the employees from his office would stop at our house at 8:15 to pick us up and dropped me off at school on the way to his office. I knew all of Telemak's colleagues. I was cute and chubby and socially precocious. Whenever I called his office, his coworker Galina would say, "Hi, Naira. Your grandfather will pick up the phone now." Galina was a very warm and friendly person of Russian heritage who grew up in Armenia and spoke fluent Armenian. Before my grandfather answered the phone, Galina and I would have brief but interesting conversations. She liked asking me questions about my school. After our chats, she would transfer the call to my grandfather, who always took my call. He was very patient and loving, always asking what he could do for me.

My grandfather's name, Telemak, is derived from the Greek mythological figure Telemachus, the son of Odysseus. His father's father, my great-great-grandfather, was a priest born in the city of Mysh in Western Armenia, which is now part of Turkey. Mysh was one of the intellectual and artistic centers of Western Armenia. Armenia used to be a large empire, independent of the Holy Roman Empire, but became part of Turkey after the genocide in Armenia in 1915.

Telemak was born in 1905 and was orphaned at the age of fourteen with four brothers and one sister. His parents died within one week of each other from typhoid. At the time of their deaths, typhoid was a common disease because there were no antibiotics to treat it.

Growing up, Telemak was responsible for taking care of his siblings. He and his siblings lived in an orphanage and went to school during the day. In the eighth grade, he walked into the office of a financial institution seeking a job. The office manager stared down through his glasses and asked the fourteen-year-old what he could do. Telemak replied that he could do anything and that he was good at calculations. The manager presented him with a book of financial transactions and asked Telemak to do the calculations. The manager said he would be back in about an hour to check Telemak's work. When he worked on these transactions, Telemak used an abacus for counting. He was finished with the assignment well ahead of the manager's return.

When the manager did return, he asked Telemak why he was not working on the assignment. Telemak replied that he had already completed it. The manager flipped through the pages, saying nothing for so long that Telemak became concerned that something was wrong. Finally, the manager turned to another worker in the office and told him he would be sent to another office. The manager then turned to Telemak and said, "You now work here."

We still have the abacus he used in his calculations.

During the 1920s, it was very common to go to university, as it was tuition free—about seventy percent of those who graduated from high school would attend after successfully completing their exams. Even though Telemak wasn't able to attend university, because he was taking care of his siblings, he educated himself to the point that he became a professional in the field of finance.

My grandmother, who was also Armenian, was born in Tbilisi, Georgia, a beautiful city full of Armenian architecture that was a center for culture and trading and served as an outlet to the Black Sea for sales from Persia. She had four sisters and one brother, and her family moved to Armenia when she was a young girl. She grew up in Stepanavan, a beautiful town in the Lori province in the mountains of northern Armenia. After she married my grandfather, she never worked outside the home, as my grandfather wanted his wife to make a good family home and to respect tradition, which included cooking and being a good housewife.

I used to love spending summer months at my grandmother's brother's house in Stepanavan. He had a beautiful yard and gardens with fresh berries. What was most exciting was that he had a cow, a goat, and chickens, which supplied warm milk and fresh eggs every day.

My grandfather and I had a very special relationship. He provided me with support, kept my secrets, and taught me how to count money. We would often go for outings together, particularly when I was young. It was very common in Soviet Armenia to have a big celebration commemorating workers on May 1, as a kind of Labor Day, with a parade in the Central Square of Yerevan. During the parade, government dignitaries including the secretary of the republic would be onstage and give the crowd a special wave.

During these outings, my grandfather and I would walk through the city to a special restaurant called Aragil, which means "stork." We would also walk to other special places in Yerevan, including a market for handmade crafts. He would buy a homemade chewing gum made from the nectar of spring flowers grown in the mountains. The gum had a milky quality, a bitter taste, and a specific smell that my mother didn't like, and she would always ask me, "How could you put that in your mouth, not knowing whose hands were making it?"

Perhaps my grandfather doted on me because my father died when I was only four and a half years old. Telemak felt that he should take care of me as my father would have. In fact, for years when I was in school and not making my own money, my grandfather would put ten rubles—in very crisp, brand-new bills—into a black wallet under my pillow every month. He said these were for me to use any time I wanted, but to make sure that by the end of the month I still had some left. He would add to the pile every month.

At the beginning of summer, my grandfather would take me to his aunt's summer house in a very mountainous region of Yerevan. My great-great-aunt's house was very old. Beautiful mulberry trees surrounded the property with blossoms that fruited in early June. There were also walnut trees that would produce walnuts in the fall. We would collect the walnuts in mid-September. Every time we took this trip to the mountains, we scaled a large hill so steep we were scared to look down, so we closed our eyes. In the distance we could see Mount Ararat. Even though Mount Ararat is now occupied by the Turks, in Armenia you can view it from the front, which is the most beautiful view, whereas the Turks see Mount Ararat from behind. Mount Ararat has two peaks. The smaller peak is called Sis, and the larger peak is called Masis. Masis is covered by snow year-round, but the snow on Sis melts during the spring thaw.

At this summer house, my grandfather's cousin directed the process of collecting mulberries. We would climb the mulberry trees, carrying blankets made especially to catch the fruit. Someone above us would shake the branches and the fruit would come showering down into our blankets. Then we would transfer the fruit to a container. In the beautiful back yard of the house was a covered grape arbor. We would sit beneath it and eat the white and black mulberries. We would spread the mulberry juice on our hands to make them silky.

I think of my grandfather every day—he had such a huge impact on my life. He would come to my performances and he knew all my music teachers, who were amazed by his dedication to his grandchildren. He would tell stories about our family over and over, including trips he and his father took to Mount Ararat. He was energetic and honest.

My brother Arthur's name came from a novel written by Ethel Voynich named *The Gadfly*, (or *Ovod*, in Russian) that my mother read as a young girl. She loved the hero in the novel and named my brother after him.

I was named after a close friend of my mother's. The legendary Nairi people inhabited the Kingdom of Urartu that stretched along the shores of Lake Van, which is now part of Turkey. This region was called the country of River, the Byzantine kingdom of Armenia, which rivaled that of the Assyrian Empire.

CHAPTER THREE

Mother

My mother, Elfreida, or Ela, was born in a city that is now called Gyumri. Previously, it was called Leninakan, or the city of Lenin. When she was four months old, my mother's parents came to Yerevan, but my mother fondly remembers spending time in Gyumri in the summertime. That was the best time of year for her because she got to spend time with one of her youngest aunts, Julia, who was only four years older than her. My mother and Julia had a special, close relationship, which they have kept up to the present time. I consider Julia my aunt as well.

Most of my mother's youth was spent in Yerevan. From years eighteen to twenty-two, she studied Russian linguistics at Armenian State University, which was very competitive. After graduating from the university, she worked for several years as a publisher at a magazine called *Reduction*, then became a member of the university's faculty.

When she was nineteen, she met my dad through a classmate and they fell in love. Mom's classmate, whom I call Auntie Aida, knew a guy named Vahan Mirakiam, who became one of the major operatic tenors in Armenia and studied at La Scala Theatre Academy. Vahan liked my mom, but Mom was not interested in him. He invited her to his singing performance, and my mom took Aida with her. Upon seeing and hearing him in concert, Aida fell in love with Vahan, and Mom was fine with that. After a few years, Vahan and Aida got married.

My dad, Alfred (Fred) Babayan, was also a classical singer, and he knew Vahan. Dad was twenty-seven and not married. It was a big concern in the Babayan family that he had not found a girl to marry. Vahan and Aida told Dad, "We have a friend you should meet, and once you meet her, you will fall in love with her. She is one of a kind. She is a very beautiful young lady, and anyone who met her would fall in love with her."

Vahan and Aida hatched the following plan: they would invite Ela to the university, and Fred would be there to meet them. If Fred saw her and liked her, he would come forward to say hello. If not, he would walk on by without stopping.

My dad was very pleasant-looking, handsome, and gentlemanly. When he came by to meet up with Vahan and Aida, he said hello, but my mother paid him no attention, so he left.

The next day, Aida told my mother, "Remember the gentleman you met yesterday? He likes you, and has fallen in love with you. He wants to take you to the movies."

My mom replied that she couldn't do that. What would she say to her parents? They were very strict, conservative, and traditional. Her mother, Vardush, was the chief on the board of education of Yerevan City. It was a responsible position. Her father, Ashot, was the director of the secret office at the radio broadcast for state security for fifty years. His responsibility was to block and control the airwaves coming in and out of the country. (Eventually a special program was developed in

Monte Carlo to allow FM radio to come in.)

Finally, Mom agreed to join Vahan, Aida, and Dad at the movies. Mom's parents didn't like Aida because she was free to go places—she was a true party girl. I think it's wonderful that Aida and my mom are still friends today.

All evening long, my dad whispered stories into my mom's ear. She decided: "That's it, I'm not going out with him." But my dad pursued her aggressively—he wanted to marry her.

During her third course at the university, my mother told Vahan, "My parents won't approve of Fred." Dad had already graduated from university and was working. Plus, he was eight years older than my mom. Vahan then pressed my mom up against the wall and put her in a choke-hold. "You'll date Fred. He's a great guy. He's very handsome."

My mom spoke to her grandmother, who said, "Let me meet him, and I will give you my okay. I'll handle your parents."

When my dad met my grandparents, he didn't know he was being scrutinized. After my grandmother finally gave her approval, Mom introduced Dad to her parents, and Dad put her parents at ease.

After dating a while, they got engaged, and before her graduation, they got married. My brother was born soon thereafter, while Mom was still in classes. She would nurse him between her classes and leave some milk for him for later. Seven years later, I was born. She was strict and focused, and worked for the state university as a linguistics teacher, focusing on methodology for learning the Russian language.

My mother and I have always had a special relationship. She found out early that I was very musical, like my father, who was very musical as a young man, and I don't remember a day that she didn't participate in my music lessons. She has the sweetest heart and is a loving, caring person—but very strict and disciplined—from whom I have learned a lot. She has no selfishness; she never asks for anything and always thinks about others. She says, "I want to be a life for you."

CHAPTER FOUR

Education

As a young girl, I loved to watch Olympic skating, and I wanted to learn to ice-skate. I was very athletic, flexible, and active, but there were no ice rinks in our area. In 1974–75, Armenia started to build professional sports ice rinks. I asked my mother, "Can I take skating lessons?"

She bought me a beautiful pair of skates. She took me to a place where they weighed me and found that I was very overweight for ice-skating. They said, "Wow—what a nice, well-fed girl." But they took me—I was ready, and I went ice-skating at that rink for a year. I was supposed to perform at an opening ceremony in the skating rink, but the ice melted and my mother said, "We are done."

At six years old, I was also very musical. I auditioned for the Tchaikovsky School of Music. They liked me and said I had rhythm, good potential, and perfect pitch. I was accepted to the school. There, I took piano lessons along with other music lessons and basic educational courses. I didn't like my first piano teacher. She wore red lipstick and a wig and looked very scary, and I was transferred to another teacher who became my mentor for eighteen years. Her name was Inessa Chuguryan.

The school was exceptional. It was not as big as some schools. I was a little naughty and very loud. I would come down from the fourth floor by sliding down the handrail of the staircase. I got into trouble and would make fun in class. For example, one day I found some smelling powder of tobacco in father's bureau. I didn't know what it was, but I smelled it and started sneezing. I thought it would be really funny if I took it to school to share with my girlfriends. After our performance, we were brought to the principal's office to face our parents. I was told that if I did that again, no matter how talented a student, I would be suspended. The principal said, "You will fly out of the school like a cork off a champagne bottle." My poor mother was so upset. I decided it was not worth behaving this way.

My math teacher, Lisa Aramovna, was the assistant to the principal. She had a lazy eye and I could never tell whether she was looking at me. She would call my mom and say, "Your daughter behaved poorly today." She was tough on me—no matter how hard I worked, she never gave me high grades. When I complained to my grandmother, she asked me, "What is her name?"

I said, "Her name is Lisa Aramovna."

My grandmother, Vardush, said, "I know her, and I'm the one responsible for giving her a job, so she'd better be nice to you." I added that she had funny eyes. My grandmother replied, "Don't say that again. It's not appropriate. Behave. It has nothing to do with your grades. If necessary, I can speak to her about your grades." But she never did.

It turns out my teacher was also working under my grandmother's supervision.

In the eighth grade, I was in love with a student who was

three years older than me. He studied violin and he reminded me of an actor I had a crazy crush on, but he didn't even know that I liked him. One day, I fell down the stairs at school and landed at his feet. He helped me up and squeezed my cheeks. "Oh, baby chubby, are you okay?" I was humiliated.

I had time outside of school for other activities. When musicians came to Armenia from Russia, we went to the concerts. We also traveled to Moscow and St. Petersburg for concerts and theatre.

At the age of seventeen, before graduation, I was getting ready for a big international competition in France in March. On December 1, a Monday, my grandparents were at home when my brother came home from the university. We lived in a big apartment in a beautiful building with beautiful verandas, but we had only two bedrooms. My brother and I wrestled in a teasing manner. He kicked me, then locked himself in the bathroom. I called out, "Seventeen plus twenty-two minus three," which is a game we played during hide-and-seek, and I punched my hand through the glass on the locked bathroom door.

I didn't realize how strong I was. I could see the bone sticking out, and blood was shooting out like a fountain. I screamed from the shock. My brother wrapped a huge towel around my hands and applied pressure. I had my robe and slippers on. We ran across the street to the hospital. My grandfather stood in the middle of the road to stop the cars so we could cross the road. I was so weak that I barely made it to the hospital.

The surgeon, whom we called Uncle Zareh, was one of our neighbors and a friend of my dad's. My grandfather told the surgeon that Fred's daughter needed immediate assistance. Uncle Zareh dropped everything to take care of me. He stopped the bleeding, took the glass out, and treated the wound. He stitched up the nerves and muscles, which required fourteen stitches.

My mother came home after work. As she walked into the living room, she saw me in the foyer with my hand on a pillow. She found it very odd and asked what happened. After she heard the story, she said, "Finally, you got what was coming to you. Are you happy now?"

After the accident, my brother felt so guilty. The healing process would take six months to a year. I was completely devastated. I couldn't wait that long. I was knocked out of the March competition, and I wasn't sure I would be able to take exams to graduate that May and enter the university in nine months.

We planned to see how far the healing had come after three months and whether I would need plastic surgery. Luckily, the nerves in my arm were not damaged, although the glass had cut some muscle. I was strong enough for physical therapy and began to work on restoring strength in my hand. The damage was not as serious as the doctors had predicted. I didn't want to lose a year—I was not patient—and didn't want to delay. You never know what might happen in a year if you aren't persistent. I worked with my doctors and fortunately had a quick recovery, but my hand never did come back as strong as before.

I never did apply for any other competitions. I was scared to apply, afraid something would happen to prevent me from entering the competition, so I focused on my schooling. And then I had a nervous breakdown about it—eighteen years of musical training down the tubes.

Fortunately, my mom and the rest of the family were supportive. I worked intensively on my piano music in anticipation of entering the Komitas State Conservatory of Yerevan in fall.

To see if I would be ready to apply to the Komitas State Conservatory, my grandfather took me to see Yuri Herabetyan, the dean of the music department. My father had taken violin at age six at Alexander Spendiarov Music School, where Yuri was a fellow student. My grandfather called Yuri, introducing himself as Fred's father. Yuri replied, "Yes, Uncle Telemak, what can I do for you?"

"Fred's daughter will apply. She is very worried about her chances of getting into the program. I want you to listen to her."

Yuri gave us an audition. Mom, Telemak, and I walked into the conservatory, and my grandfather greeted Yuri as Yuri Grantovich, his formal name.

It was very straightforward. He said, "I am ready whenever you are."

I was very nervous. I asked, "What should I play?"

He replied, "Chopin's Étude in G-flat Major."

When I finished, he said, "Now play the next étude." This étude had originally been scored by Paganini and transcribed for piano by Liszt.

Yuri got closer to the piano and gave me advice. He asked me to continue. This time I played a sonata by Beethoven. For nearly an hour, he played the same music at the other piano.

My grandfather finally asked Yuri, "Does she have hope?"

He replied, "Yes, she's going to get in. Let her try out."

Then I played again. He said, "Yes, you can sit for the exams."

At the exams, there were nine to twelve jurors, including the rector at the conservatory, Lazar Manterosovich Saryan, the son of the great Armenian painter, Martirose Saryan.

I passed my exams with straight As.

When I finished playing, I was asked questions about the professional music world.

"Sing the main entrance to the opera *Norma*."

"Who is the composer?"

"What was the main role in the opera?"

"What happened in the opera? Describe the libretto of *Norma*."

"Describe Mozart's *Magic Flute*."

"What happened during the *Magic Flute*?"

"Tell me how many parts there are to Brahms's second concerto."

I got straight As and then played at the colloquium as part of the oral exam.

I went to the fourth floor elated. Seven more exams to go, including solfège (theory), dictation, oral exams, a Russian essay exam, an oral Russian literature exam, and a history exam. There were nine exams altogether, and in August of 1984 when I went to see the list of students who had passed the exams, I found my name, Naira Babayan, on the list. I was so happy to see it there. My wish came true.

On September 1, I walked proudly to the Komitas State Conservatory of Yerevan. It was an honor to study at the conservatory. Being accepted meant I had special talent and skills as a musician. It was a chance to study at a high-level school. Graduation from this school would also give me a direct entrée to continue my study in Moscow. The doors would be open anywhere I wished to apply.

CHAPTER FIVE

Music Conservatory

At the Komitas State Conservatory of Yerevan, eighteen of my twenty-five classmates had graduated with me from the Tchaikovsky Music School. I had studied with them for twelve years. It was great to be able to continue with them, and I was looking forward to starting classes on September 1.

We had a very interesting ceremony to open the year. The rector of the conservatory stood by the door to welcome the new students to the first course. It was very pleasant and unusual, and the best experience that anyone could have had.

For the first time in my teenage years, I was exposed to new freedoms. The standard age for a high-school graduate was eighteen, but my school had one extra year because it was a special school. Students at other schools graduated in ten years; in my school, students graduated in eleven.

The first part of the day was for practice. There were big piano studios on the third floor of the building. Our lectures began at 1 p.m. in the auditorium. We studied philosophy, history, and the science of communism. For that class, my grade was a C, and I wanted a B, as I was an

A student in everything else, but I wasn't studying. Isabella Ilichna was my history professor. She was very proud that she was born in 1917, the year of the Russian revolution; in 1984 she was sixty-seven years old and she had never married. She liked me, and I liked her. She was sharp, educated, and very direct with us, but she had a sense of humor. I took her classes for two years.

She told me, "If you study certain paragraphs and get an A in the exam, your final grade for the class will be a B."

For the sake of my mother's hard work, in honor of my father, and out of respect for my father's position as secretary of state, I studied hard for a week. But when I took the test, I cheated. I had written the answers on my hand. I couldn't remember all the answers, as I had missed a lot of the classes and had not spent a lot of time on my homework. My newfound freedom had taken time away from my studies.

I also used certain memory guides to remember certain themes—the works of Marx, Engels, and Lenin, politics, and continuing the ideas of Marx and Engels.

The rest of my classes were in philosophy, aesthetica (the study of beauty, emotion, sensation, and behavior, as opposed to intellectuality), polyphony, music history, and European, Russian, Armenian, and modern history. All of these concepts were very important to the study of music.

Aesthetics helped me by teaching me to portray and convey the beauty of the music. It also helped me in my performances.

Methodica was a course about the music itself—how to express music and the method of music.

The second course of the year was called Practica Prepodavania, the practice of pedagogy, in which the professor invited children to sign up for piano lessons and taught us how to teach them to play. I got an A on the exam in the master class and received a special certificate with my diploma.

The graduates of conservatory receive a master's degree after five years of study. For those five years at the conservatory, I took piano lessons early in the morning for forty-five minutes twice a week, followed by one to seven ninety-minute lectures in the afternoon.

At nineteen years old, I was becoming a pedagogue and a student of practica at the conservatory. It was a very busy time. At the same time, I was studying accompaniment, ensemble, performing, and generally learning to become an intelligent musician.

Yuri Hayryapetyan was my pedagogy teacher and coach, and I thank him for that.

CHAPTER SIX

Earthquake

In early December 1988, Armenia was in conflict with Azerbaijan over Baku. Gorbachev was acting like a jerk by not supporting Armenia. There were annual parliamentary meetings of the Communist party to talk about what should be done during the year. And I was completing my fourth course at the conservatory.

On December 7, 1988, at 12:15 p.m., I was preparing to go to lectures for the afternoon. My brother was at work. My mom and Telemak, who was eighty-three years old, were at home. Telemak was sitting in the foyer waiting for me. I was in the bedroom with my mom.

First we heard a weird sound. Then the house started shaking, and we could hear clinking noises. There was a lot of crystal in the house—the chandeliers, the whiskey bottles. The floor shook under our feet. I yelled to my mom to crawl under the table or stand under the doorframe.

This went on for a minute—a minute that felt like it would never end. I couldn't get my mother's hand—it pulled away from me.

Then the shaking stopped. I didn't realize what it was. Then it started again.

The earthquake in Armenia killed over 25,000 people and destroyed many cities. Its epicenter was two hours away, in the city of Spitak. My mother's hometowns, Leninakan and Stepanavan, suffered major damage as well. Spitak was very seriously harmed, with houses, hospitals, and schools leveled to the ground with the people still inside them.

Electricity, telephones, and all lines of communication to the cities were cut off. When I called Aunt Julia in Gyumri, she didn't answer.

At 4 p.m. my brother said, "I'm going to Gyumri to see what has happened." He was twenty-six years old. We didn't know what he would face on the roads, but he set off after work an hour later. We lost contact with him until he returned because there were no cell phones and no communications. We later learned that when Arthur got on the road, he got stuck in a huge traffic jam and was not able to reach Gyumri until midnight. The city was totally dark, and people were yelling and screaming. He had never seen such a scene. He was speechless—so much death. There were people alive who seemed dead—they were in shock. People were hanging from collapsed buildings, screaming. People were searching for family members at schools and hospitals, but their family members were all gone.

Because of shoddy construction, the buildings had collapsed like cardboard houses. Widespread corruption in the construction industry had resulted in substandard buildings, but this earthquake was 9.9 on the Richter scale. It is possible that even buildings built to code would not have been able to withstand this earthquake, which had not been foreseen.

All my mother's relatives—my aunt, my uncle, their daughters—lost their houses. My great uncle's daughter and her three daughters disappeared.

Aunt Rima, the eldest aunt, was at work when the earthquake struck. Aunt Rima worked at the agricultural institute as a researcher. She lived alone in an apartment and supported herself by growing vegetables in a garden nearby. One day when she was walking home along the railroad tracks with a suitcase of potatoes, five wild dogs attacked her. She crawled to the first house she could reach to ask for help getting to the hospital, where she received special shots in her stomach. Her legs had been all torn up and she was infected with rabies for almost a year.

When the earthquake struck, Rima ran from her office to her house, where the only thing left standing was the refrigerator. She ran to her brother's house, where the earthquake was still going on. His four-story house was very old and well-constructed. Her building had collapsed.

My cousin's husband was searching for his wife and their children around a building that looked like a hill of rubble. Miraculously, he heard sounds coming from underneath the rubble. He called out their names, not knowing whether it was his family. With the help of others, after several hours he was able to find a way to rescue them. My cousin was found underneath the building with her three baby daughters, where they'd been for nine hours. She had covered them with her body to protect them. Her spine had been broken and half her face was gone. Dust and dirt had blinded her babies, but the girls survived because they took shelter beneath a table and were not smashed.

When Arthur came back to Yerevan, his face was green. He couldn't speak. They took my cousin on a stretcher to the hospital. My grandfather sought out the same surgeon who had worked on me when my arm was cut by the glass. My cousin survived, and her face was saved by grafting flesh from elsewhere on her body. There was a big scar near her eye, but luckily, she didn't lose her eye. The hospital was also able to restore her children's eyesight. We took care of her for a while in our house.

The earthquake was a horrible tragedy. Many people lost close relatives, but the whole world supported us. Many countries, especially the United States, Soviet republics, France, and Canada, came to our aid. Charles Aznavour, a popular singer and diplomat who was born in Paris but of Armenian heritage, was considered an Armenian hero for his efforts. Every other week, he traveled to Armenia with food, clothing, and other essentials. During the winter, he sent airplane loads of warm clothes, blankets, food, and dry goods to the earthquake victims. The government in Moscow was doing everything it could to help.

I still had a half year left until graduation in June of 1989.

CHAPTER SEVEN

Graduation

After five years of intensive study, in 1989, the day of my graduation came. For my major final exam for piano performance, a teacher from Moscow Conservatory came to serve as the chief justice to evaluate the students. Her name was Vera Gornostayeva. (*Gorno* means "mountain" in Russian.) She was a Russian pianist and pedagogue. She was a graduate of the Moscow Tchaikovsky Conservatory.

My program included a prelude and fugue from the *Well-Tempered Clavier* by Johann Sebastian Bach, two Chopin études, Schuman's *Papillons*, and a Beethoven concerto. I was very stressed. A lot was hanging in the balance. This was the conclusion of five years of study at the conservatory, my last opportunity to shine. I wanted to be able to pursue my double master's in Moscow. If I was not good enough, I would not be able to do so.

I was very nervous. My left foot shook on the left pedal as I played my piece. I tried to control myself. Finally I brought myself into the right balance. As I finished my performance, I heard applause that I was not expecting. At first I thought they wanted me to stop. Then I turned my head to the right. Gornastayeva stood up and applauded.

"This is the kind of student we want to hear." She thanked me.

I came down the stairs and shook her hand. The rest of the judges congratulated me. They told me to wait behind the door with the other students. I didn't know what the results of the final exam were; other students still had to perform. Then they would announce the results.

There were five categories of results: Category 5 was an A; Category 4 a B; Category 3 a C; Category 2 a D; and Category 1 an F, presumably a failing grade. The names were announced alphabetically. Three students started with a B. I received a 5, or an A.

I was very proud, fulfilling my mother's dreams. I could go to conservatory. That day, walking out of the building, I knew how to play and perform. I was given a referral by Gornastayevna to study in Moscow tuition free. I wouldn't have to pay a penny.

It was very difficult reaching this point—not everyone was able to accomplish the goal of continuing their musical education. Like getting into Juilliard, it was a privilege to study at the state university. It was very special to study there with support from parents, grandparents, and teachers.

It was May 1989, and I was twenty-two years old. I had started in 1984 and had completed my college education. I was headed for the Moscow journey.

CHAPTER EIGHT

Moscow

When I finished my last exams early, I was referred to the Gnessin Academy in Moscow to study with Professor Gambaryan for my master's degree.

In order to study in Moscow, I would need a place to live—either an apartment or the dormitory at the academy. That February 1989, my brother had a business trip to Moscow and decided to take me with him. When we were leaving for Moscow, he asked my mother if she had Uncle Kamo's telephone number. Uncle Kamo was one of my father's closest friends, a surgeon and head of the hospital in Moscow. We had not seen him since my father died. My brother decided: "We will call him, if he's there."

We flew to Moscow and stayed at the Hotel Rossiya on the western side of the city overlooking the Kremlin. When we arrived, my brother placed a call. "Hello, Uncle Kamo, this is Arthur Babayan."

There was astonished silence at the other end of the line. Then, "Arturchik, where are you?"

"I am here, with Naira."

"Are you in Moscow?"

"Yes."

"We will see you tonight."

We got his address, which was right off of the Mayakovskaya Metro station, on Gorky Street. It couldn't have been a better location in Moscow.

That evening we rang the bell at their house. When the door opened, Kamo and his wife, Aida, were standing there, speechless. We received a warm reception. They couldn't stop looking at us. "I'm looking right in front of me at Fred's two kids."

Kamo had two sons, Armen and Nikolai. They were very nice and polite. Armen was a medical school graduate. Nikolai was a young diplomat. I sat between them, receiving the very best treatment. I liked Nikolai—he was young and attractive. It was very sweet watching the two brothers compete for my attention, but of course I had no intention of being serious with either one at that time. Nikolai was ready to get married; I found out later that by law you couldn't go abroad to serve as a diplomat without having a family.

The next day I received a phone call from Nikolai. He was inviting me to dinner, but both brothers came to dinner. A few days later, I got an invitation from Armen to go to a movie. When I went with him to the movies, he gave me a letter. It was a love letter, which I read when I returned home to Yerevan. I didn't know how to respond to the letter.

After I returned to Yerevan, I told Kamo and his sons that I had been accepted at the academy in Moscow. Kamo said, "You will stay with us for two years." My mother agreed. That summer, I flew to Moscow to start school in the fall.

In September 1989, I began my two-year graduate program. There was a lot of work: study, research, and pedagogical work. My program was to become a concertmaster and a piano accompanist. Every semester I would advance to the next step. My program consisted of playing the music of certain composers, mostly in chamber music groups consisting of violins, cellos, and ensembles. I learned how to listen to the other musicians. I had to know how to balance my playing with the soloist's without dominating.

School started at 1 p.m. for five to six hours of classes. I took the trolleybus to class. The professors and instrumentalists would wait for me. I was preparing a program to perform for the judges; with that performance I would earn credits and advance in the program.

When I moved into Kamo's house in Moscow, I felt pressure from Armen to enter into a relationship with him. He had told his parents that he had written me a letter, and he became very insistent. His parents wanted him to give me an engagement ring because I was not supposed to be with someone unless I was engaged.

We were good friends, but I wasn't crazy about him. However, I was not allowed to show my feelings. I was having a good time in Moscow, and it was gracious of the family to host me in memory of my father. I told my mother that I didn't like Armen, but I thought I would grow to like him if I spent more time with him. I continued my studies, but the situation distracted me a lot.

I told Armen, "Let me finish school, and I will decide what to do."

Even though this issue took a lot of concentration away from my studies, I finished early because I wanted to go back to Armenia. That summer I finished my exams, and by November 1990, I had received my second master's degree at Gnessin Academy.

When I was leaving Moscow, Armen came to the airport and begged me to stay, saying, "I love you." He didn't want to lose me.

I was very straightforward. I told him, "I never loved you. No, I'm not coming back." He was heartbroken, but I knew I didn't love him. I returned the ring to him.

Armen's family was not pleased. They felt I had taken advantage of them. It became very ugly.

Perhaps, in retrospect, I could have been more diplomatic, but the situation drove me to that point, to be straightforward and leave.

CHAPTER NINE

Albert

At age twenty-three, I applied for a job at the Komitas State Conservatory. They called me right away and asked me to work in the Department for Concertmasters. I accepted, and in that position I taught young students to accompany or play ensemble with singers and string musicians. Interestingly enough, I was working with professors I had studied with when I was younger, and I was still learning from them. I was living at home and feeling secure.

The end of 1990 and the beginning of 1991 was the worst time for our new republic. Armenia was already in bad shape politically, as it was seeking independence. When the Soviet Union collapsed in 1991, each republic was free to attack other nationalities within their borders. The neighboring republic of Azerbaijan began persecuting Armenians. In Baku, the capital and largest city of Azerbaijan, Azerbaijanis were killing Armenians who lived in Azerbaijan.

Once Armenia gained independence, all gas and electricity that flowed into Armenia was shut down, so we had no energy during the winter of 1990–91. It was horrible. We had no heat and no plumbing. My mom and I didn't shower for three months that winter. We went to bed in our clothes—it was six degrees Celsius inside and minus fifteen outside.

For four years we had no heat or plumbing. We would walk within our house in our boots and coats. We heated water on a small kerosene lamp like a Bunsen burner. The stores were empty. We would get up at four in the morning to get in line to buy bread with coupons.

During the blockade that winter, I was still performing music. One day I was performing at the Architecture Union Auditorium. It was eleven or twelve degrees Celsius. We were lucky at that time and had electricity, but everyone brought candles in case the lights went out, as they frequently did. The lights would be shut off in one region so they could be turned on in another region for a while. Five minutes into the performance, the lights shut off.

Everyone was very supportive. Two people held candles next to me, and in the audience, people held lighters. Everyone was quiet, listening to me with great appreciation. I played for an hour and fifteen minutes, straight through without intermission. I was exhausted and cold. Right before the end of the piece, the lights turned back on for five minutes, then off again.

The person who arranged these performances introduced me to an Armenian man who looked at me with surprise and great interest. I felt that he was attracted to me. His name was Albert. He had arrived from Glasgow and had established a business in Armenia.

Albert grew up in an Armenian household in Tehran. At seventeen he left Tehran to study at the polytechnical department of Glasgow University to become a mechanical engineer. After spending time in England, he returned to his hometown to be closer to his parents. When we met, he had an opportunity to develop a business in Armenia.

He introduced himself very politely and moved on. He was very nice. The next day I received a call from my producer saying, "This guy is in love with you." I found him very attractive—he reminded me of Omar Sharif. Albert asked me to have dinner with him. I agreed because the place where we were meeting was warm and there was electricity. After some time we became good friends. We dated briefly and decided to get married. We did not need much time to decide, as we felt very comfortable with each other.

Albert was a bit older than me and he had a big family that I adored. They were all very kind to me. They were from the capital in Tehran, where many Armenians live. Before Khomeini, the shah of Iran welcomed Armenians. It was the best place in the East to live. It was a great life at that time. After the revolution, life in Iran changed. Many Armenians left, although Iran still has a large Armenian community. We stayed in Iran during and after our wedding, as Albert's family lived there. It was a pleasure to spend time there.

A year after we were married, Mariam was born. I was twenty-five years old and over the moon with Mariam. I adored my daughter. Although she was born blonde, she now has jet-black hair. I remember playing with dolls as a child, wondering when I would become a mother. It became real with Mariam.

We were happy, but heading into tough times. It was cold and there was nothing to eat. I would give Mariam a bath in hot water in the sink because it was the smallest space to warmly bathe a child. I was performing and working at the Pedagogical University, teaching at the Armenian

State Pedagogical University in Yerevan. I squeezed in hours part-time at the conservatory in the Accompaniment Department.

During that time, two-year-old Mariam's tonsils needed to be removed because they were frequently infected. We had planned to travel in December to see Albert's family and have a real wedding reception with the whole family. After Mariam's tonsils were removed, Albert insisted that we travel by car rather than fly. I didn't know what I was getting myself into. It was very dangerous to travel through a mountainous region in the snow. We put snow chains on the tires of our small Italian Lada and stopped in the city of Megree (which means "honey") in Armenia on the border with Iran, where we stayed overnight with some of Albert's friends. The next morning, we drove to the border—about a thirty-minute drive—and parked our car near the Arak River so our friends could take it back to their house. It was winter and very cold. Mariam was covered with a huge blanket. As we walked over the bridge to Iran, the river splashed our feet.

At the other end of the bridge, a car had been sent to pick us up and drive us to a hotel. We were in Old Tabriz, a city outside Tehran. We were all exhausted. My mother was furious. She said my husband was not acting responsibly, that he should have told us what was involved in the trip. Traveling from Tabriz to Tehran would take another eight hours. We should not be driving; we should fly instead, she said. Albert was very apologetic and agreed.

We changed our plans and arranged to fly to Tehran. The moment we arrived at the airport, the stewardess asked whether we were ready to come off the plane in Tehran. I would have to cover my head, and my coat had to come down to my knees. The airline provided me with a scarf. I felt the presence of that country's traditions.

Fifty people, including aunts and uncles from my husband's family, came with gifts and flowers and balloons to meet us at the airport. Mariam was taken away from me and swept up into the bosom of Albert's family.

The wedding plan was to drive five hours from Tehran to a semiautonomous city on the Caspian Sea called Haykashen. Most Armenians there have houses—it was a Christian Armenian city that allowed Armenians to walk around without head coverings. No Muslims could enter. A lot of Armenians traveled there for the holidays; they still do. My in-laws had villas in that town. There was a church with a big hall prepared for the wedding. I had already been married by law, but my in-laws wanted us to have a real wedding in an Armenian church. They were taking all the wedding food with them from Tehran.

I was very tired from the trip, but I had no dress for the wedding, no real ring, and no shoes. Everyone but Albert, his sister, his cousin and I had left for Haykashen. We ran around Tehran from shop to shop. We bought a beautiful dress. The shoes were one size too small, but we had no choice with no time left. The next day, I dressed up for the five-hour trip to Haykashen.

On December 31, we had our wedding in Iran. I was twenty-seven years old. Mariam was the center of attention. She was shocked and crying. It was a very emotional time and very loud, and she was very tired.

CHAPTER TEN

Dubai

We had a great wedding. It was fun, with lots of dancing, kindness, and beautiful, warm memories. I loved these people very much. I never thought at the time that I would divorce Albert later.

The next day, January 1, I woke up around 11 a.m. Albert was not there—he had gone hunting. It was his big hobby. He brought back two fat wild pigs he could sell to a buyer. On a big table in the yard, Albert dressed the pigs himself, skinning and cleaning them with a huge knife. When he was skinning the pig, his knife slipped, cutting off two knuckles. He put ashes from his cigarette on the wound, wrapped a bandage around his hand and held it tight to stop the bleeding, then kept cleaning the animals. He was a man of extremes who took big risks. That's probably what ended up breaking up our family.

After ten days, he left for Armenia for business. We stayed in Tehran for two months because it was so cold in Armenia and Mariam was still recovering from tonsil surgery. We returned to Armenia in March. Life was going on; we flew back.

It was 1994. Albert was trading with companies in Iran, bringing back eggs and clothes to sell in Yerevan. I was taking care of Mariam and working at the conservatory and the Pedagogical University. We wanted another child, but it was not happening.

Five years after Mariam was born, I began to feel that something was different, and soon learned that I was going to have another child. I felt so blessed. I kept playing in Yerevan and performing. The electricity would work for a very short period before going out. We used kerosene heaters to heat our house.

At the time, Albert was in Dubai doing business. No one knew about the UAE in Armenia. The UAE was only about twenty-five to twenty-seven years old, and there were huge reserves of oil that were instrumental in the development of the country.

Right before my thirtieth birthday, Joann was born. I was expecting a boy, but it was a girl that cried. I felt like the luckiest woman in the world. When I saw her, she was perfect. Other mothers came to see this perfect baby. She was always petite, and looked as perfect as if someone had painted her. She had a beautiful face, with dark hair and darker skin, like her father.

By that time, Albert had a good trading business with Iran. He was one of the first Armenian businessmen to establish a business in Dubai. He was a caring father, kind and open. He was very generous. I had great relationships with his family. When Joann was born, Albert's mother, Marie, was very kind to us. She came to visit us. When Albert traveled to Dubai, he brought back many toys for Joann, plus disposable diapers—Pampers and Huggies—which we could not get in Armenia.

One day he asked me, "Would you like to live in Dubai?" I asked what it was like there. He told me it was a great life, lots of fun, lots of facilities. He was describing paradise. I trusted him completely. We finally decided to travel there when Mariam was five and a half and Joann was one and a half, and in November 1997, we moved to Dubai.

My brother wanted to travel with us to help us settle in a new country. When we arrived in Dubai, it was one hundred thirty degrees Fahrenheit. In early November, the humidity level was one hundred percent in the Persian Gulf. Living in Dubai was difficult. I had two babies and did not know the Arabic language. We had lots of belongings, and we were staying at the Sharjah-Emirates Grand Hotel, in an extended-stay residence that had a kitchen.

One day, when Albert and Arthur went to the office, I was depressed. I didn't know how to operate the air-conditioning. I started to cry.

After one week, my brother left to take my mother to Los Angeles, where he lived. That was a horrible day, but he told me, "Everything will be fine—we'll bring you to the States."

The next day, Mariam got very sick due to the extreme differences in temperature between the heat outside and the air-conditioning inside. She had chronic bronchitis and her lungs were not strong. I waited a whole day for Albert to return so I could shop and cook and take care of the babies.

"How long are we staying in a hotel?" I asked him. "We need to look for a home."

We started to look. Mariam turned six on November 22, and we finally found something cheap, in a new development near an artificial lake called Sharjah Corniche.

CHAPTER ELEVEN

Apartment

We slowly started moving in to our new apartment, but we had no furniture. We had nothing more than clothing, kitchen stuff, and not much money, as we were on a limited budget. We started looking for a TV and furniture for a small living room and one bedroom. Joann, Albert, and I slept in one bed, and Mariam slept on the pullout sofa in the living room. Prices for furniture were cheap and reasonable, for the time being.

My brother stayed there while we settled in. He shared certain concerns with Albert about Albert's business, but I was not involved with any of this business. It bothered me, but I didn't argue with Armenian men, especially my husband and brother. I wish that I had.

One day, Albert, the kids, my cousins, and I decided to visit Jumeirah Beach Hotel, an unusual luxury hotel that only the Arab world of wealth could create. It was absolutely fantastic—the service, the luxurious rooms, the beauty of it. We stayed overnight in an economy suite that cost about $1,000 a night. I never found out who paid for it; perhaps it was a gift from my brother. We had a great time. The kids loved the Gulf—they didn't want to get out of the water. The next morning, we had a beautiful breakfast buffet. It was great fun. It seemed we were looking through rose-colored glasses. Everything appeared to be washed in a pink light.

That evening when we returned home, my cousins stayed in the car while my brother, Albert, and I went upstairs to the apartment. I don't remember who put the key in the door, but we couldn't open the door. There was a huge sound. Arthur pushed hard with Albert's help to open it.

The whole apartment was flooded. It was like a swimming pool, with water twenty inches deep throughout the apartment. There was a cement floor underneath the rug. The workmanship was so good that the water couldn't escape from the apartment. Our clothes and furniture were soaked. The shoes were floating like boats. My brother's fancy Bally shoes were ruined. We ran downstairs to tell my cousins to come up. Everyone panicked. It's possible Albert forgot to shut off the bathtub spigot. We were never sure. We tried not to accuse each other of causing the flood. We treated it as a kind of comedy, to keep our spirits up.

That night, we took the kids to my cousins' hotel room, and we stayed up all night waiting for the manager's office to open in the morning. We worked to get as much water out of the apartment as we could. In about two hours, the emergency service came and used a special vacuum to suck the water out. Giant hoses pumped the water into a huge van outside the building. We stayed in the house and opened all the windows for the carpet to dry.

After two days, Arthur left Dubai, but I wasn't sure why. I suddenly felt very lonely, very foreign, and very uncomfortable in the place I was living, because Albert was out of the house most of the time.

CHAPTER TWELVE

Learning Dubai

Here I was, alone with two young girls in a tiny apartment in a strange Arab country. I would do my best to make sure my girls were safe and well cared for.

I wasn't working. I was a full-time housewife and mother. I decided to leave for Armenia and stay there from June to September because of the intense heat in Dubai during the summer months, and because I wanted to see my family, and because Albert was working all the time.

We decided to find a school for Mariam when we returned to Dubai. We found the Victoria English School, a British school, and I signed her up for the fall term. The school agreed to use the textbooks I gave them so that she could learn her lessons in Russian as well as in English. In September, we returned to Dubai. Albert called my mother, who was back in Yerevan, and invited her to come back to Dubai with me and the kids. My mother said, "I'm working. I can only come for a month."

When we arrived at the airport in Dubai, Albert said, "I have a surprise for you. We're taking a different road home." We stopped in the parking lot of a building I'd never seen before. He said, "This will only take five minutes. I want to show you something."

We took the elevator up to the sixth floor. We walked along a bright, airy corridor to an apartment on that floor. Albert opened the door, and I saw this beautiful place already furnished with our belongings.

"You're at home. Welcome home," he said.

While we were in Armenia, Albert had gotten a new apartment and new furniture and moved our belongings into it. I was very happy—and astonished. It was the last thing I expected. It was very nice of him. The kids jumped up and down. They each had their own room. Joann had been sleeping with us in a little bed.

The apartment was clean, spacious, and in a nice location. Albert's office was closer. This got me into a better mood. To be honest, I still didn't know what my husband did for a living. I had an idea that he did some trading, but I didn't know with whom. A local sheik had sponsored us into the country, but I didn't know who.

My mom stayed with us for about a month and a half. Mariam was now in school.

Albert was the only one who drove because I didn't have a license in the UAE. I needed someone to help with the kids so I could learn the language, so I wouldn't be at home all the time. After a while, I couldn't take it anymore. It was very difficult to push Joann's carriage around in the hot weather—around forty-eight degrees Celsius, or one hundred eighteen degrees Fahrenheit, plus one hundred percent humidity. My mother got a substitute professor to take her place at the university so she could come back to Dubai for two months to take care of Joann while I went to driving school and English class.

When I started attending English class, Albert said, "I'll get you a taxi to take you there." After a long trip around town (the cab driver had difficulty finding the place), I arrived at the school late. I opened the door and saw a woman who looked European but was dressed in Pakistani clothes. I asked her if I could sit next to her. She replied "Yes" with a very distinct accent. At the break, we introduced ourselves. Her name was Yvette, and she was from Budapest. She was married to a Pakistani with whom she had a child. She was a lovely lady. We became good friends and have remained so to this day. I was very pleased to come to class to learn basic English. My English was very poor.

One day, Albert had a meeting at the Bank of Sharjah. When we walked into the bank, we were invited to the president's office. When the secretary ushered us into the office, a gentleman stood up. I gave him my hand. He asked the secretary to bring us coffee. He was very handsome and had very gentlemanly manners, and was dressed so well. At some point, I excused myself and waited outside. The gentleman invited us to dinner that evening. I didn't have anything to wear to meet a special high-level Sharjah sheik, so we went shopping.

We went to the City Centre, a shopping mall I was not familiar with. We went into a beautiful shop called Massimo Dutti. I bought a very pretty summer dress with a jacket. At the dinner, I met the president's wife and a couple of Armenians who worked for him. We stayed for the reception and dinner, but didn't stay long.

One day my mother said, "We have some nice neighbors. Yesterday in the foyer, I met a young lady who started talking to me. Her name is Sonya, from India. She has a young boy. It will be great for you to get to know her. She speaks English and she is your neighbor. I'm going to find the Armenian community here."

When my mother told me there was an Armenian community, I realized we would find the community at the St. Gregory Church. The Blessing of the Church was coming. Also, Sunday school and Islamic school were on Fridays. Thursdays and Fridays were the weekend. The work week began on Saturday.

I went to the church and spoke to the principal of the Sunday school. The school had many Armenians from all over the world, including the United States, Canada, Lebanon, Syria, and Iran. We were probably the first Armenians from Armenia. I registered Mariam for school there.

However, there was a problem. The language they taught in the school was based on the language spoken in Western Armenia, whereas our family was from Eastern Armenia. I asked whether the school would teach Mariam in Eastern Armenian if I brought her books to the school—the same material would be covered, but the program would be a little different. The principal agreed. I was grateful and relieved. I was very pleased with my progress, and that my mother had pushed me to meet the Armenian community.

And now that I had taken steps forward with school—learning the language and taking the driving course—I had to learn the rules of the road.

Standing from left: Naira's great grandfather Mnatsakan (Babayan), Mnatsakan's two brothers (Telemak's uncles), 2nd row seated from left: Mnatsakan's wife Haikanush with youngest child, Telemak, Priest (center) and Telemak's aunt, 3rd row from left: Mnatsakan's children on left, Telemak's uncle's children to right

Seated center:
Great grandmother pregnant with grandmother Astghik
Standing on either side:
great aunts on Babayan side of the family

Astghik and Telemak

*Great grandmother Sirun (means beautiful) and
great grandfather Sedrak Kardashian
Kardashians are on mother's side – related to
Robert Kardashian*

Ela (Kardashian) & Fred Babayan (1958)
(Elfrieda & Alfred on passports)

Arthur, Telemak & Naira – 1972
Telemak in middle, Arthur on left, Naira on right

A FAMILY PORTRAIT

Naira and Arthur (1973)

Naira playing the piano as a child (5 years old)

Ela & Naira (6 years old)

Godparents & children, Naira, Ela & Arthur
Raffik standing rear (godfather)
To his right, Mary (godmother)
To Mary's right, her daughter
To Mary's daughter's right, Ela
To Mary's left, Arthur
To Arthur's left, Mary & Raffik's son
Between Arthur & Mary, Naira (in braids)
To Naira's left, Raffik & Mary's youngest daughter

To right – Ela
To left – Arthur
Bottom Naira (6 years old)
Ela cut Naira's hair because
Naira was giving Ela
a hard time.

Naira (7 years old) in park
in Gyumri
Photo taken by Ela's
Uncle Gregory

Naira in Yerevan in front of Mt. Ararat

Meeting with Denis Matsuev after concert at Strathmore

Naira performing at the Church of the Epiphany, Washington, DC

Naira performing at German embassy 2017

Naira holding flowers after Van Cliburn concert

Annie Totah, Placido Domingo, Naira

Annie Totah, Queen Pahlavi and Naira

Naira and Mariam

Joann & Mariam in bathtub in Dubai

Naira, Mariam and Joann in Yerevan just before coming to the United States to live.

Mariam in decorative jacket in Washington, DC.

Joann at her graduation from University of Maryland.

CHAPTER THIRTEEN

Living in Dubai

People started coming to see us, and we were getting to know the community. Albert was not sociable, so the responsibility for meeting with people rested with me. The Armenian community was small and tight-knit. They were curious to meet us as newcomers to their community.

When the church was blessed in 1997, the pastor came to our house. After Easter, it's traditional to invite the pastor to bless your house, so we did. The pastor blessed the water, salt, and bread. After lunch, he asked me, "What do you do?"

"I am a professional musician, a pianist," I replied.

"That's great, and good to know." He asked me, "Naira, would you take on the responsibility to play the organ on Friday and establish and conduct the Armenian choir at the church?"

What he was asking was a big obligation and responsibility, and I had two little children at home. Then I thought, "Why not?" The children could be involved, too. Albert could come and take care of them at the church.

I said, "I will give you an answer in a few days."

He replied, "You are a very diplomatic young lady." I was just thirty years old.

I talked with my mom, who said, "Of course, Naira, don't even think about it."

I called the pastor. "Yes, I will be there." There was just one problem: I had to find time for rehearsal. We decided to rehearse on Tuesday evenings. The pastor's wife sang with the choir, and she had a beautiful voice. I discovered that I could sing well, too, and we sang together. The music for our first performance was based on a liturgy by Komitas, an Armenian composer, and Vardaped, an Armenian priest.

Two weeks later, our new choir had our debut at the church. I sang along with the choir. I was very nervous, but it went well. After that, people got to know me. People were curious to know who this organ player and singer was. I was making my introduction to the Armenian community. From then on, I was very welcome in the community.

Every Friday morning like clockwork at fifteen minutes to eleven, the Father would come out for the service, which would last two hours, then we would have lunch. We would talk with people. It was a warm atmosphere, especially during the Christmas and Easter holidays. The religious holidays were times to celebrate.

Joann was always right next to me, but Mariam was hard to keep at church. After school, Albert was helpful and supportive. He was quiet and had a smile on his face.

I was concerned about Joann. She was already two years old and not talking. She was saying only "Mama," so I was very worried. I realized I needed to find a doctor for my children, so I asked people for a referral. I went to a clinic and found a doctor named Ardemis. She was an Armenian from Syria who had studied at the Yerevan Medical University in the 1960s.

When I went to see the doctor, she said, "Don't worry, she will talk. She's not ready yet." Shortly, she began to speak words, and about six months later, she was talking.

Dr. Ardemis had a daughter, Nairi, who was graduating from high school. She played the piano. When Dr. Ardemis learned I was a musician, she asked, "Will you teach her to play piano when you come to our house?"

I gave her lessons in the evenings while Albert watched the kids. I took a taxi to her house, and after her lesson, Nairi would drive me home.

We started talking. "Are there any other musicians around here?" I asked.

She gave me some names. "Carmen is a girl from Lebanon. She studied in Yerevan." It turned out Carmen was the same girl I had studied with at Yerevan Conservatory. Carmen contacted us. She was very pleasant, and it was cool to see her ten years later. She had established herself in Dubai. Her husband was working at a company owned by a relative. She registered as a teacher at Trinity College London in Dubai. She told me, "They will accept you at the college as a piano teacher."

I interviewed and got the job. They were charging good rates, and there were good students there. For my lessons, I charged $100 per hour.

Carmen was a very sociable woman. We got along well. We would have picnics together when the weather was pleasant and barbeques at the parks. We had a good time.

I also met Aline, an Armenian who was very Lebanese, at the church. She had twin boys and another boy. Aline became my neighbor.

I also met Lena. She was the assistant to the principal of the American University of Sharjah. She became very interested in me as a professional musician. She asked whether I would be interested in performing at the American University. I instantly accepted—without remembering that I did not have an instrument to practice on at home.

Albert and I found a music store in Dubai that sold pianos. I purchased a beautiful upright piano. The piano was delivered, and after adjustments, tuning, regulating, and voicing the instrument, I began to practice.

Shortly thereafter, I received a formal invitation from the American University in Sharjah to perform there. The university did not have a grand piano, just an upright. My husband said he would buy a grand piano for my performance. I needed a grand piano, anyway, for practicing.

We worked out a deal with the university for them to rent it from me. So, my husband bought a Yamaha grand piano, which was delivered to the Armenian University in Sharjah for my performance there. The piano was affordable, about $5,000. I had about four to five months to develop a beautiful program for a full solo performance at the university.

CHAPTER FOURTEEN

Performance

I needed a dress for my performance. Apart from the performances at the church, this would be my first professional performance in the UAE. I went to a shop in Dubai that had all the popular name brands. Then I went to the Salvatore Ferragamo store. I saw this dress that was so simple, but so beautiful. It was short-sleeved and made with fantastic material. When I saw this dress, I wanted it. I also needed shoes and accessories, and I got them all at once. It was meant to be.

It was 1998, and this would be the first professional performance I had given in two years. I was very nervous. The dean of the university, who was also a professional architect, introduced me onstage. My program included Beethoven's *Pathétique*, Chopin nocturnes, some waltzes, and Ballade No. 1 by Chopin. I played the first part before the intermission. At intermission, my mom came up to me and found I had warmed up and was much calmer.

Following intermission, I played Chopin's Ballade No. 1. After my performance, I was so relieved. I thought, "Oh my God, it's over." Then someone approached me from behind to congratulate me on my performance. It was the general manager at the Bank of Sharjah, to whom my husband had introduced me when we first went to the bank. He said "Apres" in Armenian, which means "Bravo." Literally, this translates to "Long life to you."

After the performance, we invited several people to our house for a reception. I became really well known at the university as an accomplished musician. I was now part of the community, but my husband didn't make any friends on his own. All who came to our house were from my circle of friends. This was weird to me. Growing up, my brother always had a huge group of friends who came to our house. It was unusual not to have friends around, but Albert didn't converse or talk much. He was very quiet, not social, which was fine after some time.

Four months later, I gave another performance. After the concert, a woman in her early fifties with gray hair and a sympathetic face approached me.

"You must be Naira Babayan."

"Yes, I am," I replied.

"You look like Naira Babayan." Although she had never met me before, she recognized me. "I heard about this fantastic performance by an Armenian woman. The way they described you, it was exactly the way you look, so I knew who you were right away."

"Yes, I am the guilty one."

At my next performance, she sat in the front row. I played an Armenian program of compositions by Aram Khachaturian. "Bravo!" she yelled from the front row.

Her name was Nora Andreasyan, and she was an astrophysicist. She worked as an assistant to Nobel Prize–winning Soviet Armenian scientist Viktor Hambardzumyan, one of the founders of theoretical astrophysics. As his assistant, Nora was a very big deal, herself.

We became friends straightaway. One time we went together to a very cool festival in Dubai called Global Village. It was full of pavilions; each pavilion was named for a country. There were many handicrafts and pieces of woodwork and furniture from India, Pakistan, Morocco, Sudan, France, and Russia representing cultural crafts from these countries. There were many things to buy, and we bought a closet armoire encrusted with handmade jewels. We carried it back to put in the car, but couldn't find the car. It was dark, very hot and humid, and our kids were with us. Finally, I just stood in one spot and said, "You go ahead. I'm not moving." My thighs were burning. Finally, after an hour and a half, the car was found. Joann was asleep in my mother's arms. She was only three years old. I said jokingly to Nora, "I don't want to see you again for some time." In part, I blamed her for the screwup, because it was her responsibility as the driver to remember where the car was. Also, her car was so tiny that I had difficulty fitting into it.

Some years later when I was in Washington, DC, I received a phone call from a woman named Anouzh whose son was interested in learning the piano. They lived in Virginia, and I replied, "I teach in DC and Maryland. I can give private lessons, but not come to your house."

"It is not convenient for me to come to DC."

A few days later, she spoke to her mother, who turned out to be Nora, who now lives in Colorado and teaches at Colorado State University. We still try to keep in touch.

CHAPTER FIFTEEN

Money Matters

We did have some nice times living in Dubai. On the eve of the new millennium, we decided to have a nice experience. Our friends from Armenia, Murad and Nune, joined us in Dubai. We spent New Year's Eve together at a beautiful Russian restaurant to usher in the New Year and the new millennium.

The next day, we decided to take a beautiful day-long tour of the desert. Once we reached a certain spot in the desert, we changed cars and got into large SUVs with professional drivers who took us into the middle of the desert. Because of the large dunes and heavy sands, driving required professional driving skills. It was a lot of fun, but also a bit scary. It was very cool, like an amusement park ride—the body of the car would go up and the wheels would stay low.

At sunset, we arrived at a tent set up for a group of tourists for a delicious dinner with a variety of barbecued items. Belly dancers came to entertain us while we enjoyed the smoke of nargile, a water pipe, a five-hundred-year-old smoking tradition. After dinner we rode camels. To get up on the camel, we had to climb on while he was on his knees, and then the camel would pull its back legs up and then its front legs. It felt like we were falling forward when the camel rose on its hind legs. It was a wonderful experience.

We went to the Jumeirah Beach Hotel on weekends because we were members. The kids loved it. It was very expensive.

Between 2000 and 2002, my brother came twice to the Emirates. I knew that Albert and my brother had a business together, but I didn't know exactly what they were doing. I became concerned that there was a serious business problem. At the same time, our relationship was declining. Albert became secretive. He had always been quiet; now he was even quieter. I didn't know what was happening with his business. He told me everything was okay, but things started getting worse. We argued about silly things—like the kids and not understanding each other. For example, Joann had a throat infection and a fever. Albert took her to the lake, not understanding that she would become sicker. When she did become sicker, he didn't do much to help her, and I had to take over.

That summer, I left with the kids for Armenia. When I came back, I sensed something was different. Albert was very quiet. There seemed to be some emotional distance between us. I didn't know what it was that was keeping him from me. I was working all day long and coming home late at night. The kids were still young, and I took them to school and to their activities. I was also teaching, practicing, learning about Arab culture, and keeping involved in the Armenian community.

My intuition is very strong. I didn't ask Albert what was wrong because I knew he was very clever, and whatever he said wouldn't be true. I began to feel something was wrong. I was not comfortable and not feeling very safe around Albert.

Because of Albert's financial difficulties, we were no longer able to afford our house and the children's private school. In March or April of that year, the principal of the school showed real kindness, as I had invited him to my performance. Out of respect for me, he let my children finish the school year for free.

I had income, but couldn't pay all of Albert's debt. I was devastated, and I didn't know what to do. Albert was distraught about his business. I lost the ground under my feet, and I decided I was only going to focus on my children at that point.

The property manager had given us one month to pay the rent or leave our four-bedroom apartment. We had been living in that place for a while. We decided to pack up and leave. We had lots of furniture. We sold as much as we could.

I couldn't leave the country for some time because of certain passport issues relating to Albert's financial difficulties, so I didn't have any choice but to involve the Armenian ambassador, who negotiated with the sheik to help us resolve these issues.

Meanwhile, Albert avoided us and tried to stay away from the house. He was embarrassed and depressed about the state of his business. He abandoned all responsibility. I was very sad for him, but at the same time I needed to be able to devote my energies to taking care of my children. I told him he needed to be strong, to be responsible, to be a man, to get himself out of this situation. He basically lost himself.

During that time, we discovered who our friends were. A local Armenian family, my neighbors, and others helped me during this time. I told my mother to take the kids while

I put our belongings in storage and I stayed with a friend in Dubai. I took my mom and kids to the airport, and I stayed in Dubai to manage things.

I received a phone call from Tehran: Albert's mother had passed away. Because Albert didn't have a cell phone, it was very difficult to inform him of her passing.

I went back to Armenia during the summer, but returned to Dubai to take care of things that were not resolved. Plus, I was trying to support Albert as much as possible. All of his deceptions about his financial difficulties and his secretive behavior had brought me to the conclusion to leave him. I obtained a divorce in Armenia and it proceeded naturally, but when I flew back to Dubai in September I decided to stay for two to three months, because I couldn't abandon Albert.

When I came back to Dubai, I stayed for a few days in a hotel until Dr. Ardemis called me. "Are you out of your mind? You must come to our house right away."

I stayed at her house for about fifteen to twenty days and shared a bedroom with her housemaid. The room was crowded with rugs she had collected on her travels.

"What are you going to do with these?" I asked.

"That's my daughter's dowry," she replied.

At the end of September, I began looking for a job and an apartment. A friend of mine, Mida—a lovely Armenian woman from Aleppo, Syria—and her family found me an apartment with two tiny bedrooms for five hundred drams (about $150) a month. It was a very good deal. With the money I had earned from selling the furniture, I rented the place, but it was full of cockroaches from the previous tenants. The apartment was difficult to clean and in a horrible neighborhood. After having spent most of my life living in more luxurious surroundings, especially in Dubai, it was a different and challenging experience.

To support myself, I found a job teaching piano privately for $112 per hour. I still had my Nissan Infinity, so I could travel to people's houses for lessons. One house belonged to a sheik who had three kids who wanted piano lessons. I made good money and was able to pay the rent and utilities.

My mother called to tell me that my kids missed me. Because Joann was very connected to me and she was suffering in Armenia without me, I flew into Yerevan and brought Joann back to Dubai with me.

Since their visas for the UAE were expiring in two years, Mariam and my mother came back and reunited with us for Christmas. For another three months, the kids were not in school.

I began to teach some of my old students to make enough money to live on, but not enough to send my kids to private school, which cost $20,000. Public schools were not an option because my daughters did not speak Arabic.

At the end of March, my kids returned to Armenia for school. At that time, I was teaching piano and was worried that I was going nowhere with my life. I would ask myself, "Why am I here?" and "Is this all there is?" I couldn't change things. The best thing was for the kids to be back at school. I felt that they should catch up on the education they had missed by being away from Armenia. Mariam was an A student in the eighth grade. She was attending Alexander Sergeyevich Pushkin School. I was worried about my kids and my mom. Armenia was very cold at that time of year and they had no warm coats. I got some clothes for Mariam from her cousins and sent clothes and money for Joann.

I already had my ticket for Armenia. I was ready to

ship a container of my belongings, which a friend had been storing for me in a warehouse. There were twenty boxes, some furniture, and the piano, all organized and ready to ship. I was very proud that I had been able to organize all of this. My mom had taken care of the kids even though at sixty-five years old, it was hard on her.

When I was ready to fly to Yerevan, I told Albert, "Don't come to the airport to see me off."

I paid another month's rent at the apartment for him and gave him two hundred dollars in cash. That would be enough for him to eat. I felt that I had taken care of my responsibilities to him, and I left thinking, *He's a big boy—he can take care of himself.* I didn't feel any guilt for leaving.

CHAPTER SIXTEEN

Back in Armenia

In 2004, two years after I left Dubai and returned to Armenia, I was thinking, "What am I going to do to get to the next stage of my life? I don't have a job. My kids are seven and twelve years old, at a new school, in a new school system. How will they handle the pressure of adjusting to this new school system?"

My girls had never studied in Russian or Armenian. Having grown up in Dubai at an English school, the transition was tough for both of them. They were very sensitive, and they had lost their friends in Dubai. I was living in my parents' house, where I grew up. The Komitas State Conservatory was ready to take me as a professor but couldn't guarantee my monthly salary. I didn't give them an answer because I couldn't survive without my monthly salary. Luckily, my cousin's mother-in-law offered me a job as deputy director of the cultural center in one of the counties in Armenia.

In September 2004, Joann was having trouble adjusting to school, and her English teacher had given her a low grade. Joann was born a leftie and she learned how to write with her left hand. The teacher, who wasn't experienced, was trying to force Joann to write with her right hand. I wanted the teacher to be kind to Joann because Joann was going through a big challenge and should write the way she was comfortable writing.

The teacher was tiny—three times smaller than me. She looked up at me as I towered over her. I grabbed her by the arm with two strong piano-player fingers, and said with a big, beautiful smile, "Madame, I don't wish to come back here to see you. Joann needs to come back with no red marks on her books (report cards). I hope we understand each other."

I realized that I was emotionally fraught. I was frustrated and concerned about my children's welfare. I think the teacher appreciated and understood my concern as she looked into my eyes. We both left in silence.

Mariam had no problems. She made friends and became an A student.

Working at the cultural center as the deputy director was a good situation until my cousin's mother-in-law, who was the director, got very ill. When she passed away, I realized that I didn't like the people who replaced her, and I didn't like the way they were running the center. It was time to leave.

I received a call from a good friend in Dubai, George Bursalian. He had been very supportive of me when I was in Dubai. He was going to visit Armenia.

I asked him, "Mr. George, if you are going to be here with your wife, Janet, I have a favor. I want you to baptize my daughter and be her godparents."

My wish was to have Joann baptized at the Ejmiatsin Cathedral, the Armenian Apostolic Church, where Mariam was baptized. The Ejmiatsin Cathedral is the Mother Cathedral of the entire Armenian Church. Armenians consider it the holiest church.

"I would be honored to do that for Joann. Get me a cross." This cross would be used in the baptism ceremony.

We went to the main cathedral in Ejmiatsin, which was almost two thousand years old. It was a twenty-minute drive from Yerevan. George came, and he became the godfather to Joann. In Armenian culture, godparents are responsible for the spiritual education of the children, guiding them to the faith.

It was the summer of 2005, and I had received an invitation to perform in San Diego. At that time, I was performing for the Armenian Philharmonic Chamber Orchestra—I had performance contracts to fulfill. But I decided to go to San Diego because the trip was a one-of-a kind opportunity. It was my first experience in the United States and my first opportunity to meet Armenian people there.

Two memorable events occurred at the beginning of the trip while I was in Washington, DC, en route to San Diego. The first was in downtown DC on K Street at the HSBC Bank. As I walked out of the bank, I found myself right outside a perfume store. I walked in and said hello to a well-dressed, polite lady in her seventies. There were a hundred varieties of perfume you don't see in other stores. I asked to try some of them. Then I heard this beautiful music and a man singing. I thought I remembered hearing that voice, but I never had. The timbre of the voice sounded familiar and the music was Armenian.

I asked the woman, "Do you know the singer?"
She replied, "Yes."
I asked, "Is it an Armenian singer?"
She replied, "Yes, his name is Vahan Mirakian."

I asked, "How do you know him? Are you Armenian?" She replied, "Yes, I heard his son singing once."

It was amazing to meet an Armenian woman in the United States who knew of my father's best friend.

The second event was an amusing one that occurred while I was preparing for my trip to San Diego. On the way to the airport in Washington, DC, I had a dress in a suit bag and a carry-on bag. However, I left my dress in the back seat of the taxicab, and had nothing to wear for the performance.

There was no time to get a dress. I spoke to the concert sponsor about it, and she said, "No problem. We'll go to Macy's when you arrive in San Diego."

I knew I would be too tired and that I would have no time to shop for a new dress when I arrived. I'd have only a short time for rehearsal and needed to concentrate on my performance. I had a light pair of chocolate-colored linen trousers, a T-shirt, and a pair of pink suede flats.

My two-hour performance included a heavy program of music by Rachmaninoff and some Armenian composers, with only a brief intermission. The air-conditioning was broken, so the hall was using fans to cool the air, but it was still very humid.

I came to the stage. People were milling about. I announced my name and said, "I appreciate the opportunity to play for you. Please excuse my attire. I left my clothes in the taxi, but here I am. Please accept my apologies." People began to clap, as they appreciated my visit from Armenia.

At intermission, I was sweating when I stood up. My trousers stuck to my butt. I went backstage and asked for a towel to put on the bench to absorb the sweat.

Eventually, I reached the end of my program. At least I didn't ruin my performance. This trip was important for my career. Another performance was scheduled in DC, but I had to decline because it was last-minute and I already had purchased my return ticket to Armenia. I was scheduled to leave in three weeks.

Everything in the United States was so unusual to me. It was a young, huge country—even the meals were large—and everything was new. People's lifestyles and attitudes were different from those in Armenia. There were lots of contrasts. I felt very foreign. Everyone spoke English, and I was extremely far away from home. I was going to museums, riding the Metro, and visiting the downtown area. The Metro in Washington, DC, was different from the Metro in Moscow, which was very old.

My mind was preoccupied with thoughts of my mom and my daughters, especially Joann, who was seven or eight years old. My mom told me that Joann was missing me. She had stopped eating and drinking, and my mother took her to the hospital for an IV glucose drip. Joann was holding my pajamas and clothes as a reminder of me and wanted me home right away.

CHAPTER SEVENTEEN

Going to the United States

I was thinking about moving to the United States, but the idea was so abstract. I was worried about my career. I was thirty-nine years old with a large professional experience behind me, but wasn't happy working for the cultural center in Yerevan. Moving to the United States would provide a chance to work in the musical profession and find better opportunities for my kids.

A good friend of my family encouraged me to emigrate, telling me that I had all the criteria to be successful as a musician in the States. My brother, who was now living in Los Angeles, tried to discourage me from coming. He said, "I can't be responsible for you, because it is going to be very difficult for you." But I told him I would do this on my own and he wouldn't need to be responsible for my success.

During that time, I received a call from Hrand Kurkjian, a friend who was working for the USAID. The doorbell rang, and an eighty-five-year-old guy was standing at the door. He was a consultant to the Armenian Ministry of Economics. He offered to sponsor me to come to the States.

I contacted my ex-husband to get approval letters to send my kids to school in DC. In November, I went to the embassy with my kids and got a tourist visa for all three of us, which was quite an undertaking because it involved arranging for my kids to enroll in school in the United States. I felt lucky to have obtained the visas. I wanted to show my kids DC during their winter break. When I got to DC, I was fortunate to meet my Armenian friend who was an American. He hosted us for six months while I applied for an immigration visa. I got Mariam enrolled in Quince Orchard High School and Joann in Rachel Carson Elementary School in Gaithersburg, Maryland. I was able to get visas for them for six months.

In 2006, I started working really hard to prepare the documents I needed for a work permit in the United States. Every step of the process required a kilo of paperwork. From March through June, I worked on referral letters (about ten to fifteen in all), then got the letters translated into English and had them notarized.

My application required that I meet six to ten criteria to qualify as an extraordinary foreign musician. I met six of them. Those who qualify for the permit possess a "distinction," a "high level of achievement evidenced by a degree of skill and recognition substantially above what is ordinarily encountered." The criteria included recommendations from noted musicians. In November and December of 2005, I had recorded a CD at the Union of Armenian Composers Recording Studio, playing a work by Frédéric Chopin. I then asked Edvard Mirzoyan to listen to my CD and provide a recommendation letter. As a noted musician, Mirzoyan's recommendation would be crucial in meeting the requirements for the application.

Mirzoyan was a classical composer and the president of the Union of Armenian Composers. He was a contemporary of Shostakovich, Rostropovich, Khachaturian, and Leonard Bernstein, and was one of their friends. Bernstein had visited Armenia several times and had become best friends with Mirzoyan.

Mirzoyan was born in Gori, Georgia. Initially schooled in music in Yerevan, he graduated from the Komitas State Conservatory and went on to Moscow to further refine his art, graduating from the conservatory in Moscow. In 1956, he was elected president of the Armenian composers' union, a position he held until 1991. He was a professor of composition at the Komitas State Conservatory, and I'd had the opportunity to meet him when I studied there. He was also a friend of my father's.

Mirzoyan was about eighty-seven years old when I called him. "Edvard Mikhailovich, my name is Naira Babayan. I am a former student at the Komitas Conservatory and a performer. Does the name Fred Babayan mean anything to you? He was my dad."

He replied, "I look forward to meeting you in about fifteen minutes."

I went to visit him. He had a beautiful house, and he was very nice to me. Because he had had a stroke, he walked very slowly. He had been a very handsome man earlier in his life, and even at eighty-seven he retained some of his good looks. He was very charismatic and professional. After that meeting, he would come to visit me at my house. My kids would help him into the house. He would sit on the sofa, grab my hand, and say, "You are so beautiful."

After the meeting, he said, "If I hadn't listened to your CD, it wouldn't have made any difference whose daughter you were. If you weren't that good, I wouldn't have been able to write you a referral."

I obtained another referral letter from Djivan Gasparyan, who, as previously mentioned, had played the duduk at my father's funeral. In time, he had become a rising star in Hollywood and was world renowned. He played with Sting, Brian May, and Peter Gabriel. His works appeared in many movie soundtracks, including *Dead Man Walking, Onegin, Russia House, Dr. Zhivago, Syriana, Blood Diamond, Gladiator, The Siege*, and *Frescos*. He also played at a commemorative service for Nelson Mandela.

I called him, saying, "I have a favor to ask." I hadn't spoken to him since my brother's wedding where Gasparyan had also performed. Without hesitation, he said, "I will meet you at the conservatory." I played for him. He said, "I don't have time to type up your referral letter. If you take my handwritten letter, have it typed, translated, and notarized, I will sign it."

By then, my file was complete. I was in a rush, because my tourist visa would expire on June 4, 2006. Finally, the immigration lawyer to whom my Armenian friend had introduced me sent the complete immigration package to the United States Citizenship and Immigration Services (USCIS, now part of the US Department of Homeland Security), which had contacted him at each step of the process. Once the immigration package was submitted, I was able to legally stay in the United States. A work permit and a social security number arrived about two months later. Then I started looking for a job.

I soon got a job at a well-known piano company, demonstrating the pianos for sale, but the owners of the store were crooks. They didn't pay me my commission on time—I had to beg them for it. The part-time job did not pay enough, so I was looking for something else. Costco was having a big demo of pianos at its Pentagon City store for two weeks. I needed the money, so I said, yes, I'd come.

It was mid-November, and I kept expecting an answer from Immigration on the status of my green card for a permanent visa. My daughters and I were living with my Armenian friend. Joann, Mariam, and I took turns sleeping on the floor and in the full-size bed. I took the bus from Kentlands, Maryland, to Metro Center in Washington, DC, to the Costco store in Pentagon City, Virginia. I worked there from 9 a.m. until 7 or 8 p.m., then took the Metro from Metro Center to Shady Grove in Maryland, where my friend would pick me up.

In mid-December, I finished that job. It was getting difficult living with my friend. He was too forward with me, treating me as a romantic interest, and I didn't want him to think I was taking advantage of him.

I kept asking Mariam to check the mail. Finally, I received two letters from Immigration. There were two cards in the letters—a card for me and another for Mariam. I called my friend Anna, who had just received her green card. She said, "Silly girl, those are your green cards." Two days later, Joann's arrived. Having the green card meant that I had residency status in the United States and could be more independent. Now I knew that I could work in my profession and be able to support myself and my children with a musical career in the United States.

I couldn't believe my relief and happiness. I went to my friend, announcing, "I got my green card."

He said, "Good for you. Now you are free. You can do what you want." He sat in his chair with his arms crossed.

I stood up, put my jacket on, and left the house.

The next day, I got my money from Costco and bought a ticket for myself and my two girls to Los Angeles to celebrate Christmas and the New Year.

CHAPTER EIGHTEEN

Teaching

My brother and his family were established in LA, and I wanted to surprise him by saying, "I'm here."

Unfortunately, I only saw my brother for a couple of hours. I wasn't able to stay with him, because he and his family were leaving for a holiday trip to Mexico the next day. Although I was disappointed, I had received a kind invitation from a childhood friend in LA, so I stayed with her and her family. It was now 2007. Joann was ten and Mariam was fifteen. We had a great time in LA and I took them to Universal Studios.

The moment I returned to DC from LA, I started applying for jobs all over town. I had already prepared letters for the music departments at the local universities.

Hrand Kurkjian saw an advertisement for the Young Artists Competition at the Kentlands Arts Barn in Gaithersburg, Maryland. He suggested that I become a member of the jury panel that judged the contestants' performances at the competition. It would be a good networking opportunity. I introduced myself to a Japanese lady named Suzanne Takahashi, who said she was happy to receive me. "We need someone to judge the piano competition." There was also going to be a string and voice competition. I was very excited to listen to the young performers, and knew that the opportunity could advance my musical career in the United States.

The Kentlands Mansion was a five-minute walk from the house. That morning, I left for the competition, which would take five hours. I was given a file with information about the competitors, what the competition was about, and how to be a judge. After judging the first part of the competition, we had a lunch break catered by Whole Foods, the sponsor of the event. There was a great variety of foods, and it was a chance to meet judges from the voice and string sections. It was a very interesting experience, judging a competition as a foreigner in the United States.

At that time, I learned about the Levine School of Music, one of the leading community music schools in the country. I soon applied to the Levine School and sent them my CD recordings. To my surprise, I received a call very soon thereafter from the chair of the piano department, Pamela Sverjensky, calling me in for an interview in August. I'd been planning a summer trip to Armenia with my kids, so I planned to return to the US at the beginning of August in plenty of time for my mid-August interview.

I was really shocked when I returned to the United States from Armenia and received a phone call from Pamela saying that she wanted to interview me that day.

It was a very stressful moment, but I said, "Sure, no problem."

My three-hour interview went very well, and I got the job as a full-time faculty member at the Levine School of Music. It was one of the greatest days, and I felt extremely happy to have made another big step forward in my musical career, one that would help me support my family.

I began working at the Levine School, where I continue to teach piano to this day. I have had very interesting, challenging, and educational experiences working in a new environment with new faculty members, new students, and a new life. At the same time, I was learning English and learning how to communicate with a new American community consisting of individuals at all stages of life, from young teens to adult students, parents, and chairs of departments. I had to make many adjustments to fit in.

CHAPTER NINETEEN

Unknown Pieces by Sergei Rachmaninoff

In 2009, I attended a performance by Denis Matsuev at George Mason University. It was the first time he had come to the United States. At this performance, he was playing Sergei Rachmaninoff's second piano concerto with the Moscow Chamber Orchestra, conducted by Vladimir Spivakov.

After the performance, I waited in line with my mom for Matsuev to sign his new CD for me. Matsuev was delayed, so the line disappeared, and the only ones left waiting were my mom and me. When Matsuev finally came out to sign the CD, we had a chance to talk because no one else was in line. He signed my CD and left.

Afterward, I was listening to the CD and heard some unknown music by Rachmaninoff. At that time, Rachmaninoff's grandson was president of the Rachmaninoff Foundation, which was located in Switzerland because Rachmaninoff had owned a villa there named Senar. The name Senar stood for the first two letters of Rachmaninoff's first name and those of his wife, Natalia, and the first letter of their surname. Denis Matsuev had recorded the piece on Rachmaninoff's piano in Senar.

I fell in love with the piece and was searching for the notes, or sheet music, but they were not available. Fortunately, I met Matsuev again by accident in Yerevan, and I asked him how I could get a copy of the notes for the unknown composition. He replied, "It's almost impossible to play it."

I replied, "What do you mean by almost?"

He asked, "Do you really want it?"

I replied, "No doubt."

I received them, thanks to my brother, who obtained the notes and forwarded them to me from Moscow.

That summer, in Yerevan, I started working to learn the notes of the piece.

The piece consists of four parts and is quite lengthy, about twenty-five pages long. According to the liner notes for Matsuev's recording, when Rachmaninoff was graduating from the university, he was supposed to write a diploma program for graduation. The professor requested that Rachmaninoff compose a piece, which he did. The piece he composed was to be performed by an orchestra, but he kept the version of the piece to be played on a piano for himself. Rachmaninoff told Natalia (his wife) that he was very tired and was not going to perform it, because there were not enough instruments in the orchestra to perform the piece. Of course, Rachmaninoff received an outstanding mark for this composition, but that was not enough for Rachmaninoff. So he sent the composition by mail to Tchaikovsky for his opinion. Because the mail was slow at that time, it took a month to arrive from Moscow to St. Petersburg. When Tchaikovsky returned it, the piece was lost, until it was rediscovered in 2007.

In 2007, Matsuev was invited by Rachmaninoff's grandson to Switzerland, who had found the notes of the piece at Alexander Ziloti's foundation at the Glinka museum.

Rachmaninoff's grandson told Matsuev, "I have something in my hands that I want you to see. I have a deal for you. If you stop smoking, I will provide you this manuscript."

Within a short time of receiving the manuscript of "Suite for Orchestra," Matsuev recorded the piece on the beautiful Steinway Rachmaninoff once received as a gift.

Since I received the notes from Matsuev, I have learned almost the entire piece, which is twenty-five pages long. This is a major accomplishment, as it is a very difficult piece to play and is not known to many other musicians. Nobody plays it because no one has the notes. It was a great honor to have been given the notes and to be able to play the piece. I've had an opportunity to give it my own interpretation.

CHAPTER TWENTY

Friends I Have Met

Besides a rewarding career teaching and performing, I have had the good fortune to get to know Annie Totah, a woman from the Lebanese Armenian community. We became close friends. She is one of the major philanthropists in the Washington, DC, metropolitan area. We went to many events together; we even took a trip together to Dubai. I thank Annie for giving me the opportunity to meet legendary musicians of the present day, including Plácido Domingo, Julio Iglesias, Michel Legrand, and Cameron Carpenter.

When I met Plácido Domingo, I introduced myself: "I am Naira Babayan."

"Oh, Babayan," he replied. "I had a singing coach for fifteen years whose last name was Babayan. Are you related?"

"No," I replied, "but that it is very interesting. I would like you to have this CD of mine, which I would love to sign for you."

He turned to his wife. "Look, Marta, I love Chopin. I can't wait to listen to it in the car. Would you keep it for me?" I treasure the memory of our first meeting.

Then, after some time, Michel Legrand was visiting DC

and performing at Strathmore with his band. I have been in love with his music since I was a teenager. On one of her visits to DC, Mom joined me at the Strathmore concert.

Legrand is a talented musician, and his performance was very impressive. Over eighty years old, he still has fantastic technique, playing and singing most of his repertoire of the songs he composed for movies. One of his band members, a harpist, had become his new wife, as he announced at the performance. I was shocked to hear someone playing the harp so well, technically and musically, in a jazz performance. It was incredible.

Mom and I decided to visit him in his dressing room after his performance. Although I wasn't sure how I was going to do it, I was prepared to give him a gift, a beautiful picture that my brother took of Mount Ararat. It was printed in a special format with explanations and certifications. The picture was quite large. I rolled it up, put it in a box, and brought it with me to the performance.

After the performance, I went to meet him in the artist's room, but security was tight. As I approached the room, a security officer said, "The artist is so tired and not able to see any people, having played two hours straight without a break."

"Shall we wait?" I asked those who were with me. "Perhaps not."

I was very fortunate that, at that moment, his wife came out of the room toward us.

"May I say hello to his wife?" I asked the security officer, who agreed.

"I am absolutely thrilled with your performance," I told her. "Is there any way that I could meet the maestro?"

"The maestro is very tired," she replied.

"Tell him that we are from Yerevan."

Her expression changed, appearing more friendly, and she went back into the room with her husband. Minutes later, she opened the door and welcomed us in, saying, "The maestro is waiting for you."

When we entered the room, Legrand was lying on the sofa. He had a handsome face, with the thickest eyebrows. I thought to myself, "Oh my God, I am standing in front of the legendary Michel Legrand."

He stood up and gave me a hug. I expressed my gratitude for his talent and his music. I told him, "I remember listening to your music in Armenia as a child. I never imagined I would be lucky enough to meet you in person." He smiled.

I added, "I would like to give you something that I think you would like."

I handed him the photo of Mount Ararat. He stood up from the sofa.

"Oh," he said, "Mount Ararat. I love Armenia."

He was pleased to receive a piece of Armenia. We rushed out, and I then realized I had forgotten to take a picture of him. But I had realized too late. His wife had left the room, and the room was locked. Oh well.

I also had a chance to meet Farah Pahlavi, the former empress of Iran, at a reception given by my friend Annie Totah. Annie had invited about 250 people to her house. I met Pahlavi's family, including her son, daughter-in-law, and three granddaughters. Annie was honoring Farah for the Pahlavis' support for the National Museum of Women in the Arts. I found Farah Pahlavi to be an absolutely humble, beautiful woman. She was a dedicated mother and grandmother. She was also a strong woman who had survived the fall of the shah during the 1979 Iranian Revolution. She lost one of her sons and a daughter due to tragic events. It was inspiring to meet such a distinguished lady who had survived a great deal and remained humble and gracious.

CHAPTER TWENTY-ONE

Performance at Steinway Piano Gallery

Right after the New Year celebration of 2016, I received an invitation from Melinda Baird, who is on the Levine School faculty and is director of education and community outreach for Steinway & Sons in Bethesda, Maryland. Melinda asked me and a few Levine faculty members to perform on a historic piano that used to belong to the legendary pianist Van Cliburn. Since then, the piano has been brought to several concert venues in the Washington, DC, area for performances of some of the most popular pieces that Van Cliburn played throughout his performing career. Right after winning the first Tchaikovsky piano competition in Moscow, which brought him worldwide fame, particularly in the United States, Van Cliburn bought that specific instrument and performed on it. It was one of his favorite instruments for performing, and it became iconic. I was fortunate to have had the opportunity to play two pieces that he performed in concert and played quite often: two preludes by Sergei Rachmaninoff. What a joy to play on that instrument.

The piano is a concert Steinway D, the largest piano made by Steinway. It was built in 1975–76 in the Steinway New York factory, completed on May 19, 1976, and given a serial number: 443530. It was inducted into Steinway's famed Concert & Artist inventory of pianos, setting its destiny for greatness. The piano performed admirably upon some of the great stages of the world, and it became a favorite of Van Cliburn's. In fact, Van Cliburn loved the piano so much that he purchased it from Steinway at the first opportunity. It was and is an extraordinary instrument; it is easy to make it sound exactly the way you want it to. I found that the instrument sounded great the moment I touched it. It is a magnificent instrument, one of a kind. It's worth $500,000, but could be auctioned for millions of dollars simply because it has Van Cliburn's signature on it.

On February 27, 2013, the legendary Van Cliburn passed away at the age of seventy-eight. After my entire performance at the Steinway concert, I thought to myself what a fortunate person I am in many ways. I never imagined in my dreams that I would be seeing, touching, playing, and performing on Van Cliburn's personal instrument. Perhaps it was meant to be that I had the opportunity to come to America; otherwise, I would not have had the opportunity to play on that instrument.

I could have never imagined coming to America and teaching others how to play wonderful piano pieces composed by such great composers as Bach, Beethoven, Mozart, Chopin, Tchaikovsky, and Rachmaninoff so others could appreciate the beauty and timelessness of music and the arts.

Yes, we have choices we can make, but there are other forces that we cannot control. Things will either happen or not. Then it is up to us to make the most of the opportunities that come our way.

As one of my dear friends said, "You can't stop; you have to move forward, and in all directions, until you find the means for self-expression and self-fulfillment."

Looking back over the many directions that my life has taken, I consider myself a fortunate person. Some of these events took a unique turn, and I guess, for good reason. I learned from those events how to live and move forward step by step. The Armenian survival genes that I have carried with me throughout my life have propelled me forward, and I will definitely pass along what I have learned to my two wonderful daughters.

Acknowledgments

I would like to express my special appreciation to Susan Silver, who was instrumental in bringing my story to publication, and her husband, Thomas Farley, who supported me throughout this project. Without their support I would never have been able to complete this story.

www.ingramcontent.com/pod-product-compliance
Lightning Source LLC
LaVergne TN
LVHW011726060526
838200LV00051B/3050

*9 7 8 1 6 4 3 8 8 3 3 6 6 *